BUFFALO'S GRAIN ELEVATORS

— HENRY H. BAXTER —

"Buffalo's Grain Elevators," originally written by Henry Baxter, was first published by the Buffalo and Erie County Historical Society (The Buffalo History Museum) in 1980 as Volume 26 in the *Adventures in Western New York History* series.

Since 1862, The Buffalo History Museum has been Western New York's premier historical organization. We are the keepers of the authentic stories that make our community unique. We tell the stories of the people, events, and movements that demonstrate Western New York's essential place in shaping American history.

Copyright © 2018 by The Buffalo & Erie County Historical Society, Buffalo, New York.
Revised 2017 by Amy Miller, The Buffalo History Museum.
Cover design by Jennifer Nichols, The Buffalo History Museum.

Aerial view of Buffalo River upstream from Ohio Street, 1924. Grain elevators are: Top left – Concrete Terminal, 1922; far left – Superior, 1918-20-22; top right – Archer-Daniels-Midland, 1920, now dismantled; above center – Marine "A," 1924; center – Perot Malting, n.d.; just right of center – American Elevator, now part of Peavey Flour Mills, n.d.; right of center – Electric Elevator, 1897. This complex is now called Silo City. Other areas to note are: Left center – The Union Furnace, now dismantled, and background – Lehigh Valley Basin, now the Tifft Farm Nature

BUFFALO'S GRAIN ELEVATORS
BY HENRY H. BAXTER

What will people of the future think of those silo-like structures standing along the waterways adjacent to Buffalo Harbor? Perhaps they will think of them as cylindrical apartment houses, abandoned by their former residents. Or will they see them as launching pads, used to send missiles on their way?

Actually, the structures are grain elevators. They stand today as symbols of Buffalo's rise and decline as a grain port. This rise and decline can be traced on the line graph printed on page 19. The graph shows the total number of bushels of grain received in Buffalo for each year between 1825 and 1975, as well as the storage capacity of Buffalo grain elevators for each year during the same time span.

Joseph Dart

THE EARLY GRAIN TRADE

Prior to the year 1827 there was no grain handled in Buffalo. Surplus grain grown in the American Midwest reached markets in the East only after transportation over long and difficult routes. Grain grown in Ohio, for example, had to be shipped on flatboats down the Ohio and Mississippi Rivers to New Orleans. There it was transferred to sailing vessels that carried it up the Atlantic coast to its eventual destination in the East or in Europe. Or it could be carried by land in wagons along the rough roads that passed through the rugged terrain of the Appalachian Mountain chain.

As an alternate to carrying raw grain in wagons, it was sometimes fed to hogs that could walk to market. Or, more likely, grain might be turned into whiskey and carried in jugs to markets on the other side of the mountains. Whichever way was chosen, transportation charges for Midwestern grain averaged $100 a ton to reach market.

JOSEPH DART'S ELEVATOR

The opening of the Erie Canal in 1825 represented a revolution in transportation. The Canal was the first efficient transportation system to breach the Appalachians. Now Midwestern grain could be shipped through the Great Lakes to Buffalo, the western terminus of the Erie Canal, and by canal boat to New York. Soon freight charges dropped from $100 to $10 a ton for grain.

There was one major difficulty, however. Even the smallest lake boats were too large for the canal, while canal boats were too small for lake traffic. Thus, grain had to be unloaded from the lake boats and transferred to canal boats at Buffalo, a process called transshipment. Handling the grain by hand was slow and inefficient, causing delays and congestion of people and boats in Buffalo Harbor. In 1830, workers handled 146,000 bushels of grain at Buffalo. Little more than a decade later, the total handled was ten times greater. At least 500 workers, most of them Irish immigrants, were required to unload or load this volume of grain by hand.

It was at this time that Joseph Dart, with the help of engineer Robert Dunbar, constructed the first grain elevator and storage warehouse in Buffalo. Begun in the autumn of 1842, it stood on Buffalo Creek at the junction of the Evans Ship Canal. Powered by a steam engine, Dart's bucket elevator raised grain from lake boats to bulk storage bins where it remained until being lowered for transshipment or for milling purposes. Some Buffalo grain dealers had doubts about Dart's innovation. "Dart, I am sorry for you," one of them said. "It won't do. Remember what I say: Irishmen's backs are the cheapest elevators ever built."

In spite of these reservations, Dart's pioneering effort was quickly and widely imitated. The pair did not file a patent for their invention. Less than fifteen years after his was built, there were ten grain elevators in operation near Buffalo Harbor. They had a storage capacity of more than 1.5 million bushels. By this time Buffalo had become the world's largest grain port, surpassing Odessa, Russia; London, England; and Rotterdam, Holland.

In a paper read before members of the Buffalo Historical Society, now The Buffalo History Museum, in 1865, Joseph Dart paid tribute to Oliver Evans as the person who first worked out the principles for handling grain mechanically. Evans, an American inventor and millwright, devised a system whereby grain was raised to a high point and then moved by the force of gravity through a series of operations. But the Evans system was used in flour mills. Joseph Dart adapted the same principles to another purpose in his grain elevator. "I believe it was the first steam transfer and storage elevator in the world," he told members of the Historical Society. "It was the first successful application of the valuable inventions of Oliver Evans to the commercial purpose for which it is now extensively employed."

The diagram shows how Joseph Dart's grain elevator worked. His first one was a primitive affair compared with what came later. "I began with buckets 28 inches apart, holding about two quarts, and raised without difficulty a thousand bushels an hour." Then, he put the buckets that scooped the grain from the boats closer together "till 1800 or 2000 bushels an hour were raised." Dart said in 1865, "In some of the elevators now in use, the buckets hold eight quarts and are only one foot apart and will raise 6,000 or 7,000 bushels an hour, weighing it correctly." Dart's first elevator had a storage capacity of 55,000 bushels but that was doubled within three years. Eventually, elevators capable of storing seven million bushels of grain were built.

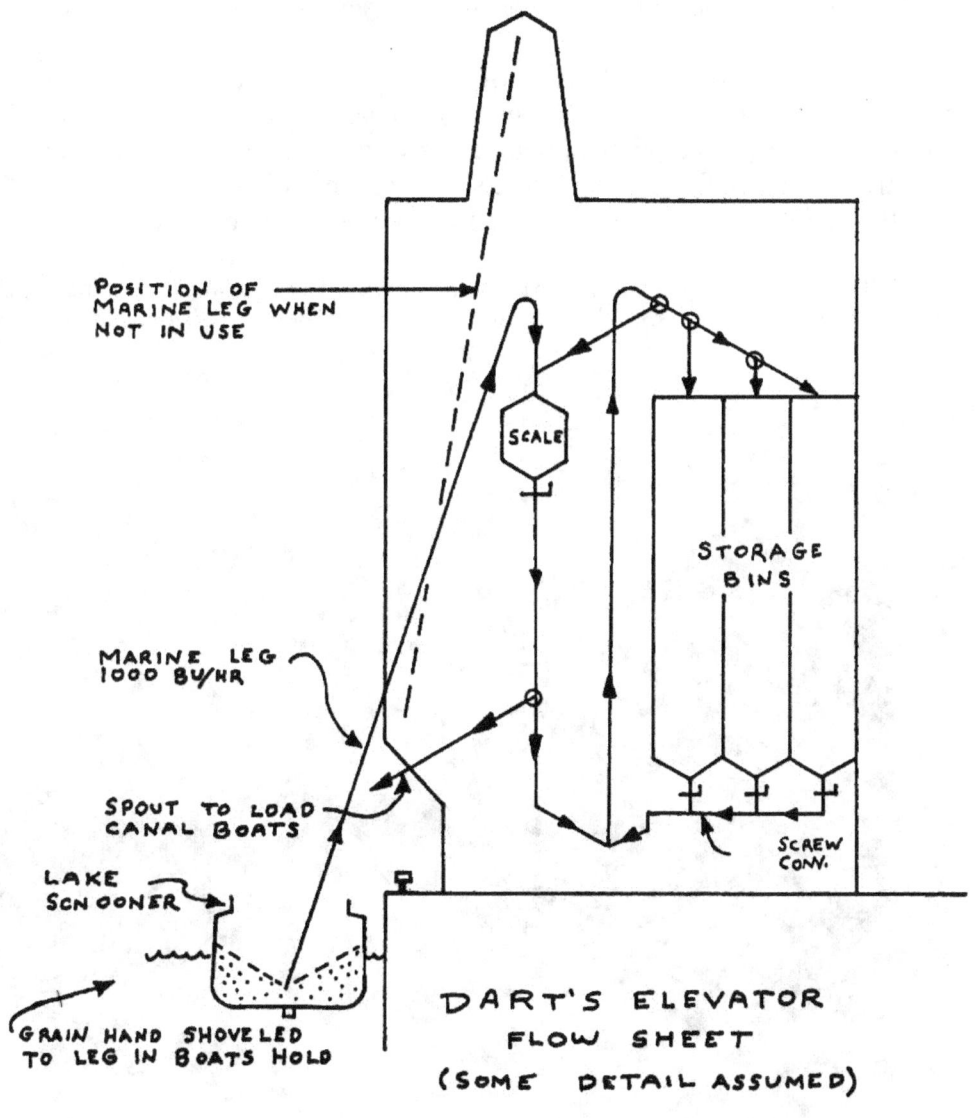

Grain elevators make ideal structures for the storage of grain. In the elevators' bins, grain can be kept dry, cool, free from vermin, and safe from pilferage. Moreover, elevators make it possible to weigh and sample grain to determine the quality, quantity, and grade as a basis of payment. Elevator-stored grain can be improved by drying, cleaning, grading, and blending. Finally, elevators can be used to assist in the milling of flour and the manufacture of animal feed and barley malt for breweries.

ELEVATORS BUILT OF WOOD

Joseph Dart's elevator was built of wood. This material, plentiful in the Buffalo area, was used for construction of grain elevators for half a century. The earliest elevators were located on or near the water and served only lake or canal boats.

A unique feature of the Watson, one of the early elevators, was a slip or waterway that led underneath it. This permitted a canal boat to be positioned inside the elevator and directly below the bins. In this way, loading of the boat could be done rapidly by gravity flow. The picture shows another distinctive feature of the Watson - the cupola on top, which set it off from other grain elevators.

The Watson Elevator had a distinctive cupola. To the left is Buffalo Creek, to the right is the City Ship Canal or Blackwell Canal. Note a typical water taxi being sculled across the creek.

Some early grain elevators had no tops on their bins, only a roof over all to keep out the rain. Explosions or fires could easily spread from one topless bin to another. Moreover, topless bins increased the chances of workers falling in, especially when they were hampered or blinded by dusty conditions.

The Wollenberg Elevator at 133 Goodyear Avenue, destroyed by fire in October 2006, was the last surviving wood elevator in the Buffalo area. The Wollenberg had an interesting beginning, being constructed from wood salvaged from the demolition of the Kellogg "A" Elevator in 1912.

In 1865, when Joseph Dart read his paper before the Buffalo Historical Society, there were 27 grain elevators built on land, plus two portable "floaters," all 29 being built of wood. Followed by a string of canal boats, floaters could travel to a lake boat in the outer harbor or in the Erie Basin. Floaters then unloaded grain directly into the waiting canal boats. Other early elevators, called "transfer towers," provided the same service as floaters except they were built on land and therefore immobile. Floaters and transfer towers were discontinued in the early 20th century.

GRAIN TRADE AT THE END OF THE NINETEENTH CENTURY

On the chart on page 19, you can see the names and storage capacity of Buffalo's grain elevators at the end of the 19th century. Only one of the transfer towers stored grain and none of the floaters did so. For this reason, they are listed separately from the other elevators. Note that the Great Northern and the Eastern had the largest capacity of all. At about this time, elevator owners charged 5/8 of a cent for elevating, weighing, and discharging one bushel of grain. The charge for storing one bushel of grain for 10 days during the navigation season was ¼ cent.

When winter put an end to the navigation season, Buffalo's grain elevators were generally full to capacity. Therefore, lake boats making their last run in the fall to Buffalo kept their grain on board until elevator space became available. Known as the "Winter Fleet," these boats made Buffalo Harbor a busy place even in the winter and spring as they were shuttled around for unloading.

Throughout the 19th century, Buffalo's grain business consisted mostly of transshipping or storage. Changes were noticeable at the beginning of the 20th century, however. Up until that time most grain shipped to Buffalo was sent on to other destinations. The only exceptions were a small amount of wheat used in the city's tiny flour-milling industry and a larger amount of barley for the numerous malt houses that supplied local breweries.

ELEVATOR STORAGE CAPACITY.

The following statement shows the names and storage capacity of several grain elevators, transfer towers, and floaters of this port:

ELEVATORS.

Name.	Capacity, bu.
Bennett	800,000
Brown	250,000
Buffalo Lake Shore Transfer	90,000
Connecting Terminal	950,000
Dakota	850,000
Eastern	1,500,000
Erie Basin (unused)	
Erie Canal (Bl'k Rock)	140,000
Evans	400,000
Exchange	500,000
Frontier	650,000
National	65,000
Husted*	200,000
International (Black Rock)	650,000
Kellogg	600,000
Lyon (unused)	
Marine	650,000
National and Globe Mills	100,000
Erie	720,000
Niagara A	800,000
Niagara B	1,200,000
Niagara C	200,000
Ontario	450,000
Queen City, A, B and C	450,000
Richmond	250,000
Schreck (unused)	
Sternberg (unused)	
Export	1,000,000
Electric	1,000,000
Great Northern	2,500,000
Swiftsure (unused)	

ELEVATORS.

Name.	Capacity, bu.
City A	600,000
City B	800,000
C. J. Wells	550,000
Coatsworth	650,000
Union	130,000
Watson	600,000
Wheeler	350,000
Wilkeson	400,000
William Wells (unused)	
Total 40 Elevators	**21,045,000**

TRANSFER TOWERS.

Name.	Capacity, bu.
Hefford	40,000
Chicago	.....
Merchants'	.....
Northwest (unused)	.....
Western Transit	.....
Raymond	.....
Total, 6 Transfers	**40,000**

FLOATERS.

Name.	
Cyclone	.....
Buffalo	.....
Free Canal	.....
Free Trade	.....
Ira Y. Munn	.....
Empire	.....
Ryan	.....
Dispatch	.....
Total, 8 Floaters	.....

* Destroyed by fire No. 23, 1899; re-building, will be finished by June.

From Annual Report of the Buffalo Merchants Exchange, 1899.

TWENTIETH-CENTURY CHANGES

During the first years of the 20th century, flour milling and animal feed industries began rapidly expanding in Buffalo. Inexpensive electrical power, first made available by the Edward Dean Adams generating plant in Niagara Falls, spurred this expansion. Inexpensive power permitted electrification of the grain elevators, which formerly had operated with steam power. The newer, cheaper power also encouraged grain processing. In addition to flour mills and animal feed industries, cereal mills and oil seed crushers became significant contributors to Buffalo's reputation as a grain processing center. By the 1930s, Buffalo stood as first city in the United States in flour milling and in the production of animal feeds from grain.

The George Urban flour mill was the first to use electric power in Buffalo grain processing. It "electrified" soon after the Adams generating plant started up in 1895. Then in 1897, the Electric and Great Northern grain elevators were built to use electric power. The Great Northern survives today at 250 Ganson Street. In this way, they eliminated steam boilers, engines, chimneys, numerous workers, and the necessity of bringing fuel to the elevator or mill site. The equipment necessary for steam power occupied separate rooms and considerable space. Now only one or two large electric motors were needed to supply power for the operation of an elevator.

The advent of the 20th century also marked the end of the use of water power in Buffalo's grain industry. Water power had been used at some of the flour mills in Black Rock that had small grain elevators as adjuncts. Those were based on the 8-foot difference in water level between the Black Rock harbor and the Niagara River. There were also grist mills at the Hydraulics, an industrial neighborhood located near Hydraulic and Seneca Streets and known today as Larkinville. These mills used water from a canal originating at a dam on Buffalo Creek. But as Buffalo turned to inexpensive and convenient electrical power, most direct hydraulic power sources appear to have ended around 1900.

Why wasn't wind power harnessed for the Buffalo grain industry? The possibility existed because there were windmills in other parts of Erie County and across the Niagara River at Windmill Point, Ontario. The answer is that wind as a primary source of power is insufficiently reliable to serve where speed, promptness, and large volume of output are essential. Windmills could be used in small operations, but they were unsuited to the large size of Buffalo's grain industry.

One more change in Buffalo's big grain business came about in the early 20th century. During earlier times, most grain came to Buffalo from the lower Midwestern states by boat. After the 1850s, much of it was shipped here by rail. But in the early 1900s, increasing amounts of grain came from the northern prairies of the United States and from the Canadian provinces across the border from them. Grain grown in these areas usually was shipped from Duluth, Minnesota; Superior, Wisconsin; or Thunder Bay, Ontario. All these locations benefited from a Great Lakes water route to Buffalo instead of the railroad routes for grain from the American Midwest. As one indication of this change, as many as 185,000,000 bushels of Canadian grain passed through Buffalo in the 1920s.

Marine leg of the Wheeler Elevator (GLF "B") built around 1906, rebuilt in 1955 to become the largest leg in Buffalo at 50,000 bushels/hour. Leg is shown on the "dip," the unloading period when a sufficient amount of grain in the hold can flow into the leg by gravity. Scooper's gear may be seen on the deck of the boat. The Wheeler Elevator survives today as the GLF at 385 Ganson Street.

HOW GRAIN ELEVATORS WORK

From the beginning, Buffalo's grain elevators were built in a variety of shapes, sizes, and functions. Still, their principles of operation were similar. And, without a doubt, their greatest days as participants in Buffalo's flourishing grain industry came during the first half of the 20th century.

Imagine a grain elevator standing 250 feet high along the Buffalo waterfront. It receives grain by lake boat. The boat is unloaded into a "marine tower" by means of a "marine leg" that resembles an elephant's trunk thrust into the hold (storage area) of the boat. Inside the marine leg are buckets attached to an endless looping conveyor belt. The buckets scoop up the grain and carry it into the marine tower.

Marine towers could be in a fixed position or moveable on wheels. Picture a 150-foot high building on wheels! With a fixed marine tower, the lake boat must be moved so the marine leg can scoop all the grain from the holds. The moveable tower can reach a number of holds, but not all of them, so some ship movement was usually still required.

Until 1864 all shoveling in the ship's hold was done manually, but in that year the power shovel first came into use. Power shovels were used to drag grain the length of the boat's hold in order to reach the marine leg. "Scoopers," or grain shovelers, operated this power shovel, but they had to shovel and sweep by hand the last grain from the hold into the buckets that raised grain into the elevator. The Buffalo grain scoopers emptied their last vessel in February 2003, replaced by automated unloading equipment.

In the early days, grain ships arriving in the harbor hired a "scooper boss," also called a saloon boss. They furnished crews of scoopers, usually 26 men, made up mostly of Irish immigrants. Usually a scooper boss owned a saloon and perhaps a boarding house. After a week's work he paid off the men in his crew at the saloon with deductions for bar bills and the boarding house if they patronized these facilities - and they usually did. As late as 1895, the average scooper earned only about $292 a year, minus deductions paid to the scooper boss. In that same year Buffalo had a high density of saloons; 7.81 saloons for every 1,000 people.

Temperance, charity, and church organizations agitated in the 1880s and 1890s for an end to the scooper boss system. Buffalo newspapers took sides for and against the situation. Finally, a long strike by the scoopers in 1899 did away with the scooper bosses. From then on, scoopers were paid directly by the operators of the grain elevators. Scoopers were still organized in crews of about 26 and were paid based on the quantity of grain handled.

In 1899, the year they organized the Grain Shovelers Union Local 109, scoopers received $1.85 for each 1,000 bushels handled. By 1935, pay had risen to $3.40 per 1,000 bushels. Still, men of Irish descent were most prominent among them. In 1940, about 9 out of every 10 scoopers was a South Buffalo Irishman.

As early as 1905, some marine legs in Buffalo elevators adopted the "pneumatic principle," a system of air flowing through a tube that sucked up grain like a giant vacuum cleaner. One large Buffalo elevator had four marine legs that could unload grain at the rate of 100,000 bushels an hour. Along with the marine leg, the marine tower contained a scale for weighing grain. There was also a device called a "lofter leg" that lifted the grain to the top of the bins and discharged it directly into them or on to conveyors. Like the elevators, these bins came in various shapes and sizes and were built from a variety of materials.

At first, bins were built of wood and usually lined with iron. After 1890, steel bins were built in a number of different arrangements. Since that time, reinforced concrete has been used. Cylindrical bins were the most common shape, though some were rectangular or shaped like a four-pointed star.

Bins holding from 20,000 to 50,000 bushels of grain were the most common size. Some smaller bins were used to house a small amount of a particular grade of grain to avoid tying up bin capacity. Monster flat-bottomed bins were built to hold up to 1,000,000 bushels of grain. Difficult to unload they were generally used to store bulk grains for an extended period.

Most bins had "hoppers" at the bottom which permitted unloading the grain into canal boats, railroad cars, or conveyors. Spouts or chutes also carried grain from one operation to another in an elevator or mill.

Grain elevators had a "workhouse" at the top, about 250 feet or more above ground level. The workhouse had room for lofter legs, shipping scales, cleaning and shipping equipment. Workers climbed ladders or rode personnel elevators to the top but both methods were costly and time-consuming. Consequently, grain elevators used an ingenious method called a "man lift." This was an endless moving belt stretching from basement to the top with 12-inch square platforms attached every 25 feet or so. To go up or down, a worker had to step on a wooden platform going in his direction and hold on.

The Standard Elevator was built in 1928. The elevator's transfer function is illustrated by the lake boat being unloaded at the same time that Erie Canal barges are being loaded.

BUILDING THE GRAIN ELEVATORS

Building Buffalo's grain elevators required special skills and a special kind of engineering. One bushel of wheat weighs 60 pounds. A 1,000,000 bushel elevator contains 30,000 tons of grain, creating an average load on the foundation of about 10,000 pounds per square foot. Land along the Buffalo River was reclaimed marshland with low load-bearing capacity. Elevators built there before the 1920s had timber piling driven down to rock or other firm material. Those supports could be from 15 to 80 feet below ground level so that the elevator would have hundreds of debarked tree trunks underneath. Away from the water, soil was better and piling not required. Moreover, steel and concrete foundations were used on some projects after the 1920s. For example, the Agway/Eastern States Elevator on Military Road, demolished in 2001, stood on a concrete mat 3 feet thick which in turn rested on a natural foundation of stiff clay.

Once the foundation was in, construction of the elevator itself could begin. In 1907, the American Elevator (now Peavey) was built of reinforced concrete. After that time, reinforced concrete was the material used for constructing most Buffalo grain elevators. Steel rods embedded in concrete provide the reinforcement. Steel keeps the bins from bursting open due to the outward pressure of the grain while concrete carries the massive loads down to the foundation. Concrete also forms a fire-resistant coating over the steel.

The "slipform method" was used to build reinforced concrete bins. At the beginning, a form (essentially a mold) usually four feet high, was built on the foundation slab. Wet concrete was poured into the form. Screw jacks placed at intervals of about seven feet were then used to raise the form. Workers operated the jacks at a rate calculated to raise the form about six inches an hour. This rate gave concrete time to harden at the bottom before being exposed by the slowly rising form.

A photo on the opposite page shows the beginning and the end of the slipform method. In the foreground, one can see the wooden form and the screw jacks in place as construction begins. In the background are nearly-completed storage bins with the wooden forms in place at the top. Using this method, it took about ten days for the Standard Elevator to reach the height of 125 feet. This was the average height of the bins. After completion of the bins, the workhouse was slipformed up until the structure reached a height of about 200 feet. Being more complicated than the bins, the workhouse was often built of structural steel rather than reinforced concrete.

The top or deck of a grain elevator under construction was an extremely busy place. Placement of steel rods, pouring of concrete, and jacking of the form were continuous processes. Generally, each jack man had twelve jacks to tend to. A whistle sounded as a signal for each man to make one turn on each jack. Raising the form six inches required 24 whistle signals each hour. During that time, a jack man would make 288 turns - almost five a minute - on his jack. Understandably a jack man occasionally got tired enough to miss a few turns. This caused his section of the form to be lower than the rest, resulting in considerable stress on the form. Such an imbalance brought distress to the job superintendent.

Supervising and inspecting the construction of a grain elevator by the slipform method was a formidable task. Concrete had to be poured properly. Steel rods needed to be placed so as to provide the required strength in the bin walls. Before construction started, workers stored sufficient reinforcing steel at the job site. After the job was completed, considerable steel might be left over, leading to the suspicion that some steel reinforcing rods were left out, possibly at critical points. According to folklore, a great deal of steel ended up in the Buffalo River to cover up omissions or implied weaknesses in construction.

Even with some truth to this folklore, structural failures were uncommon. Fires, explosions, and collapses for other reasons occasionally did occur. These incidents provided some of the most dramatic events in the history of Buffalo's grain elevators.

Hecker-Jones-Jewell Elevator being built using the slipform method, 1928.

SPECTACULAR EVENTS

Fire destroyed a number of the early wooden elevators. Newspapers related the story of when the National and Globe Elevator on the Evans Ship Canal burned to the ground on a Sunday in October 1963. The National and Globe was built one hundred years before and was out of use at the time it burned.

After the 1890s, construction with steel and reinforced concrete reduced the problem of fire, except in the grain itself. Spontaneous combustion of grain may cause a slow, smoldering fire deep in the interior of a bin. Using water to douse the fire would spoil the unburned grain, so other methods were developed to deal with this problem. The bin may be "turned over;" that is, the grain run out to another bin to cool it off or dry ice can be placed on top. This process generated heavy carbon dioxide gas that sank into the grain and smothered the fire below.

The Ontario Elevator on the Evans Slip Canal after it collapsed in 1904.

Grain dust can explode violently. One such explosion occurred in 1913 at the Husted Mill and Elevator. The explosion killed 33 people and injured 80 others. Agway "B", one of the first concrete elevators built in Buffalo, has topless bins, like some of the older wooden elevators. When Agway "A" and the Eastern States elevators were built, they had individual concrete covers for each bin. The theory was that in case of an explosion, a cover would blow off without disturbing the other bins, much as a safety valve protects a steam boiler. In this way designers of the elevator hoped to limit damage from an explosion. Even so, such a cover (actually a concrete disc 20 feet in diameter and weighing 4 tons) would cause considerable harm if blown into the air. Fortunately, no explosions occurred at Agway "A" or the Eastern States and none of the concrete tops were lifted forcefully from the bins. The explosion relief idea was not tested.

Exact causes of fires or explosions were sometimes difficult to determine. Sparks from electrical equipment and static electricity built up on moving belts were blamed. Overheating of poorly adjusted or badly aligned machinery caused fires. Careless smoking was a hazard.

As years passed, safety and health measures reduced dangers. Specially built enclosures prevented the escape of sparks or fire from electric motors, switches, and lights. Smoking was strictly controlled. Workers wore face masks to guard against inhaling grain dust. Cats attacked hungry rodents while fumigation took care of invading insects.

Modern grain elevators included other ingenious devices that improved safety or health conditions. Among these were temperature sensing devices consisting of cables in each bin. They relayed dangerously high temperatures to a central point so action could be taken in time to prevent spontaneous combustion or other damage to the grain. Some large bins had ports near the bottom through which air was blown to cool off the grain.

Dust control equipment and explosion suppressors became increasingly important. Noise of operations, distances of hundreds of feet, and grain handling rates of from 10,000 to 30,000 bushels each hour made rapid, accurate communications essential.

In spite of all these precautions, small accidents and occasional large ones did occur. For example, in 1973 an explosion badly damaged Pillsbury's bulk flour storage bins. This catastrophe put the mill out of operation for more than a year.

Husted Mill and Elevator explosion, 1913. It was later rebuilt as the Superior Elevator, which still stands at 874 Ohio Street.

To the left is the almost complete Spencer-Kellogg Elevator, now St. Mary's Cement, which replaced the Coatsworth Elevator in 1909. In the center is the Kellogg Wood Crib Elevator "B." Note the "Turret" Style vessel from Newcastle, England being unloaded.

DECLINE OF THE GRAIN TRADE

Buffalo's grain trade reached one of its high points during the 1920s when receipts exceeded 300,000,000 bushels a year. World War II, plus the necessity of helping to feed western Europe in the post-war years continued to stimulate the grain trade. As a result, the late 1940s saw several years when grain received at Buffalo elevators and mills approached or exceeded the 300,000,000 bushel level.

Since that time, the loss of Buffalo's grain industries was severe. Many grain elevators were abandoned or are being used to less than their full capacities. Elevator storage capacity declined from a high point of 58,400,000 bushels in 1942 to a low point of 22,650,000 bushels. The winter fleet that once numbered hundreds of vessels is now extinct.

The reasons for this decline are complex but three of the most significant are clear. The Welland Ship Canal (the fourth one built in the Welland, Ontario, area) opened in 1932. With its opening, full-sized grain boats coming from upper Great Lakes ports could by-pass Buffalo, delivering their cargo to Prescott, Ontario or Oswego, New York, for transshipment. Virtually no Canadian grain has been transshipped from Buffalo since that time. Next, completion of the St. Lawrence Seaway in 1952 gave moderate size ocean vessels access to the interior of North

America by way of the Great Lakes. This ended Buffalo's grain transshipment business completely.

While the transshipment business was coming to an end, Buffalo's animal feed industry was likewise declining. Decentralization occurred in this industry during the years between 1955 and 1970. Grain and other animal feed ingredients were no longer shipped to the large feed mills in Buffalo. Instead, smaller mills were built within trucking distance of the regions in which cattle, hogs, and horses consumed the animal feed. As a result, nearly all of Buffalo's feed mills ceased operation. At one-time, Buffalo's mills annually ground over 100,000,000 bushels of grain and other ingredients into animal feed. With the feed industry gone, Buffalo's grain traffic suffered yet another drastic decline.

A ship in the Buffalo River is unloading at the GLF (Agway) Elevators "A," "B," and "C."

The Great Northern Elevator, built in 1897 by James J. Hill, is an adjunct to the Pillsbury Flour Mill. It is a unique design with steel bins enclosed in a brick sheath.

The end of transshipment and the loss of the animal feed business meant more than a decline in the grain trade. It meant a serious loss of jobs. At one time, thousands of men and women worked in some capacity associated with the grain elevators and the grain business. Now their jobs are gone.

Buffalo remains prominent only in the milling of grain into flour. Even this prominence is threatened by new developments in transportation and business organization. Buffalo badly needs a modern Joseph Dart to apply new or even old technology to enhance the natural advantages that a large lake city has.

Years ago, the poet Carl Sandburg wrote that fog comes "on little cat feet" and sits looking "over harbour and city on silent haunches" before it moves on. Buffalo's grain industry was bustling and noisy, not silent like the fog Sandburg wrote about. Moreover, unlike the fog, Buffalo's grain industry left evidence of its presence "over harbour and city." The last vessel to have grain scooped by Buffalo shovelers was the S.S. Kinsman Independent in 2003.

Grain elevators and mills, even those now empty and abandoned, are the evidence of the time when Buffalo's grain industry flourished - and then moved on.

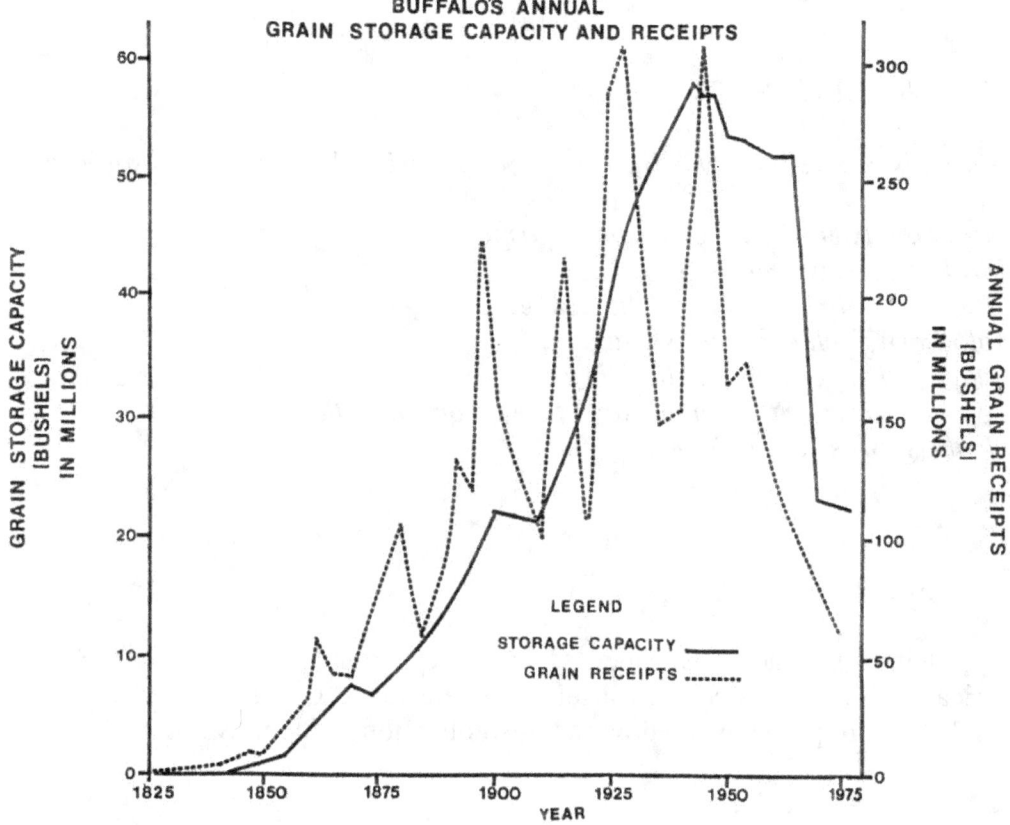

ABOUT THE AUTHOR

HENRY H. BAXTER, P.E., a graduate of Cornell University and a licensed professional engineer, was employed as Associate Engineer by the Plant Department of the Buffalo Board of Education since 1968. From 1946 to 1968, he was associated with the A. E. Baxter Engineering Company. From its founding in 1896, this company specialized in the design of grain mills.

He served on the board of directors of the Canal Society of New York State and is a member of the Society of Industrial Archaeology. With Erik Heyl, he coauthored *Maps, Buffalo Harbor 1804 - 1964*.

ACKNOWLEDEGMENTS

Harold Ahlstrom & Laurence Burke – Buffalo Harbor Museum, suggestions and editing.
Edward D. Baxter, review construction aspects.
Gloria I. Baxter, typing.
Dr. Richard C. Brown, suggestions and editing.
Buffalo Corn Exchange, statistical data.
Buffalo and Erie County Public Library.
Lockwood Library, State University of New York at Buffalo.
Wollenberg Bros., data on their elevator.

BIBLIOGRAPHY

Leary, Thomas E., Sholes, Elizabeth C. & Healey, John R. (1998). Historic American Engineering Record: Buffalo grain elevators. Buffalo, N.Y. Retrieved July 17, 2018. http://www.loc.gov/pictures/collection/hh/item/ny1667/

www.ingramcontent.com/pod-product-compliance
Lightning Source LLC
Chambersburg PA
CBHW081135180526
45170CB00008B/3116